STARS OF HIP-HOP

DRAKE

RAPPER AND ACTOR

BARBARA GOTTFRIED

Enslow Publishing
101 W. 23rd Street
Suite 240
New York, NY 10011
USA

enslow.com

This book is dedicated to Joe Roda, a Drake fan and the funniest person.

Published in 2020 by Enslow Publishing, LLC.
101 W. 23rd Street, Suite 240, New York, NY 10011

Library of Congress Cataloging-in-Publication Data

Names: Gottfried, Barbara, author.
Title: Drake : rapper and actor / Barbara Gottfried.
Description: New York : Enslow Publishing, 2020. | Series: Stars of hip-hop | Audience: 2 | Includes bibliographical references and index.
Identifiers: LCCN 2018046437| ISBN 9781978509573 (library bound) | ISBN 9781978510098 (pbk.) | ISBN 9781978510111 (6 pack)
Subjects: LCSH: Drake, 1986—Juvenile literature. | Rap musicians—Canada—Biography—Juvenile literature. | Actors—Canada—Biography—Juvenile literature.
Classification: LCC ML3930.D73 D74 2018 | DDC 782.421649092 [B] —dc23
LC record available at https://lccn.loc.gov/2018046437

Printed in the United States of America

To Our Readers: We have done our best to make sure all websites in this book were active and appropriate when we went to press. However, the author and the publisher have no control over and assume no liability for the material available on those websites or on any websites they may link to. Any comments or suggestions can be sent by email to customerservice@enslow.com.

Photo Credits: Cover, pp. 1, 17, 23 Andrew Chin/Getty Images; p. 5 Skip Bolen/WireImage/Getty Images; pp. 7, 8 George Pimentel/WireImage/Getty Images; p. 11 Thaddaeus McAdams/WireImage/Getty Images; p. 12 Kathy Hutchins/Shutterstock.com; p. 14 © AP Images; p. 18 Johnny Nunez/WireImage/Getty Images; p. 21 Prince Williams/WireImage/Getty Images; p. 25 Justin Sullivan/Getty Images; p. 27 Splash News/Lotus House/Newscom.

CONTENTS

THE BEGINNING OF A RAPPER

Drake is now rich and famous. But his early life was not easy. Aubrey Drake Graham was born on October 24, 1986, in Toronto, Canada. Drake's dad is named Dennis. His mom is named Sandi. Drake is both black and Jewish.

Drake was five years old when his parents got a **divorce**. His dad moved away. Drake stayed with his mom in Toronto. His mom worked hard, but they did not have a lot of money. First, they lived on Weston

Road. It was a poor area. Then they moved to a richer part called Forest Hills. Drake and his mom rented space in someone's home.

Special Times

At thirteen years old, Drake had a Jewish ceremony called a **bar mitzvah**. At thirty-one, Drake had another bar mitzvah party. His mom, dad, and friends came.

GOING TO WORK

When Drake was about fourteen, his dad was in jail. There his dad met someone named Poverty. Drake and Poverty shared their raps. **Rap** is a kind of music with words, **rhythm**, and a beat.

Drake went to two high schools. Some students bullied him for being half Jewish and half black. And his mother was sick.

"One of the greatest feelings in my entire life. As of tonight, I have graduated high school!"[1]

Drake wanted to make money to help out. When he was fifteen, he quit school to work. He wanted to act on TV.

Drake's mother was a teacher. She did not want her son to quit school. Drake promised his mom that he would

Drake and his mother attend the 2011 Juno Awards in Toronto, Canada.

finish high school someday. He kept his promise. At twenty-five years old, Drake earned his high school diploma.

Drake and Shane Kippel (*right*) starred in the show *Degrassi: The Next Generation.*

CHOOSING MUSIC

At the age of fifteen, Drake began acting on a TV show called *Degrassi: The Next Generation*. Drake played a character named Jimmy Brooks. He was a basketball player. On the show, Brooks was shot by another student. After the shooting, Brooks had to use a wheelchair to go places.

Drake wanted to act and do music. He spent all day acting on *Degrassi*. After work, Drake played music. Finally, Drake had to choose between acting and music. He chose music. Later, Drake did a music video for his song called "I'm Upset." It included people from his old TV show.

IT'S A RAP

Drake's dad played the drums. Drake's uncle Larry played another instrument called the bass. Music was in Drake's family. Drake made a **mixtape** with a lot of songs. It was called *Room for*

Ways to Listen

Albums and mixtapes both have songs. Albums cost money to buy. Mixtapes are usually free. People could get *So Far Gone* for free.

Improvement. He also made another tape. It was called *Comeback Season*.

Drake's third mixtape made it very big. It was called *So Far Gone*. It had two hit songs. The songs were "Best I Ever Had" and "Successful." After this mixtape, record companies wanted to sign a contract with Drake.

Here, Drake's dad, Dennis Graham, joins Drake for the 2016 Summer Sixteen tour.

Drake appears at the 55th Annual Grammy Awards in California in 2013.

WINNING AWARDS AND TOURING THE WORLD

Drake signed a contract with a record company. Then he made his first album. It was called *Thank Me Later*. It sold a lot of copies.

In 2010, Drake also went on tour. He went to different places in the world to sing. Drake sang to students at colleges in the United States. He also had a big concert known as the OVO Fest in Canada.

Drake later made a second album called *Take Care*. Many people bought this album, too. *Take Care* even won a Grammy Award for Best Rap Album in 2012.

One song on *Take Care* won an MTV award for Best Hip-Hop Video. *Take Care* is an emo album. Emo rap is a kind of music that talks about feelings. Some of the songs on *Take Care* tell about how Drake feels about fame and love. He also sings about the struggle between wanting things and having them. Other songs talk about the battle between dreams and real life.

In 2011, Drake signed autographs in Toronto before *Take Care* came out.

ARTSY ALBUM COVERS

Drake's next album was *Nothing Was the Same*. *Take Care* and *Nothing Was the Same* have art on their covers. The cover of *Take Care* shows Drake looking alone and thinking. He's thinking about how his life changed after becoming famous.

The cover of *Nothing Was the Same* shows

"Sometimes, it's the journey that teaches you a lot about your destination."[1]

Drake at two different ages. It shows him as a baby and as an adult. This art stands for his past and his present.

KEEP IT COMING

Drake had more top albums. His next one was called *Views*. It has songs about the seasons in Toronto: winter, spring, summer, and fall. There was a girl named Megan Flores. She was dying of cancer and wanted to meet Drake. He granted her wish. Drake said the *Views* album was for Megan.

Views helped Drake win many awards. He won thirteen at the Billboard Music Awards. "One Dance" was a popular song

Drake wins a Top Billboard Album Award for *Views* in 2017.

from the *Views* album. It was played more than one billion times on **Spotify**. Spotify is a music streaming service. It is like radio on the internet.

ANOTHER HIT ALBUM

Drake's next album was *More Life*. Kanye West worked on this album with Drake. It has many different music artists, such as Young Thug, Lil Wayne, and

Drake and PartyNextDoor at the Sound of Brazil in New York City on October 23, 2014

PartyNextDoor. The song called "Glow" had eighteen artists, songwriters, and producers working on it.

The album also brings together different countries. It has a song about a South African leader named Nelson Mandela. It also has **dancehall** music that comes from Jamaica. Even the title of the album comes from a Jamaican saying. "More Life" means "to wish someone well."[1]

Hoops and Rap

Drake loves basketball. He talks about some famous basketball players on his *More Life* album. He mentions Kobe Bryant and Michael Jordan. Drake cheers for the Toronto Raptors.

SONGS OF TRUTH

In 2018, Drake had his next biggest hit. It was an album called *Scorpion*. The songs on this album talk about many things. Drake talks about having a son. His name is Adonis. He was born October 11, 2017. Drake

"Live without pretending, Love without depending, Listen without defending, Speak without offending."[2]

also talks about how people's feelings can get hurt. The album even has a song for Drake's mom.

This album has two sides. One side has rap. The other side has music called **rhythm and blues**, or R&B for short. Seven of the songs on this album made

Drake performs on the 2018 Aubrey & The
Three Amigos tour in Chicago, Illinois.

the Billboard Hot 100 Top 10 chart. From
all his mixtapes and albums, Drake has
had 31 top ten hits. He beat famous singer
Michael Jackson's record.

DOING BUSINESS AND GIVING BACK

Drake has a company called OVO. This stands for October's Very Own. Drake's birthday is in October. The symbol of the company is an owl. In 2011, OVO started a clothing brand.

In 2012, Drake and two friends started OVO SOUND. His friends' names are Noah "40" Shebib and Oliver El-Khatib. This company makes and sells music from different artists. It also sells clothes that features these artists.

OTHER BUSINESS VENTURES

Drake has millions of dollars. He makes a lot of money from his music. He also makes money from his OVO clothes business. Drake **invests** money in other places, too.

Drake performs at the Hard Rock Hotel and Casino in Las Vegas, Nevada. The OVO owl is behind him.

Investing means putting money into things that will hopefully earn more money. Drake has invested in Virginia Black Whiskey and the Toronto Raptors NBA team.

Drake also earns money by being in ads. He has done ads for Apple products, Nike shoes, and Sprite drinks. The Sprite ad begins when Drake is trying to record a song. He then drinks a Sprite and it helps him figure things out better.

Blogs and Fests

Drake has an OVO blog that shares songs, videos, and pictures. He has also done OVO Fest since 2010. It has different popular musicians each year—including Drake.

Drake wears a jacket with the Apple company symbol at a 2015 Apple event. He high-fives Apple's senior vice president Eddy Cue.

HELPING OTHERS

Drake grew up with a mom who had trouble paying the bills. He became a famous music artist who made millions of dollars. Over the years, Drake has helped other people that need money.

"I like it when money makes a difference, but don't make you different."[1]

Drake has given money to schools, children without homes, and people living in poor neighborhoods.

In 2017, Drake helped people that were hurt by Hurricane Harvey. In 2018, Drake gave away almost $1 million to places in Miami, such as a high school, the fire department, and a homeless shelter.[2] This

Drake donates $50,000 to a women's shelter
on February 8, 2018, in Miami, Florida.

donation was part of the "God's Plan" music
video. Drake continues to use his fame and
money to make people's lives better.

TIMELINE

1986 Aubrey Drake Graham is born October 24 in Toronto, Canada.

1999 Drake has his bar mitzvah at the age of thirteen.

2001 Drake first appears on *Degrassi: The Next Generation*.

2006 Drake releases his first mixtape, *Room for Improvement*.

2010 Drake releases his first album, *Thank Me Later*.

2010 OVO Fest premieres in Toronto, Canada.

2013 *Take Care* wins Drake a Grammy for Best Rap Album.

2013 Drake becomes global ambassador for the Toronto Raptors basketball team.

2017 *More Life* gets more than one billion streams in the United States in April.

2017 Drake wins thirteen Billboard Music Awards.

2017 Drake's son, Adonis, is born October 11.

2018 Drake releases his double album, *Scorpion*.

2018 Drake gives away almost $1 million to help those in need.

CHAPTER NOTES

CHAPTER 1. THE BEGINNING OF A RAPPER

1. Gil Kaufman, "Rapper Finally Graduated from High School After Dropping Out to Be in 'Degrassi,'" MTV News, October 18, 2012, http://www.mtv.com/news/1695780/drake-high-school-diploma/.

CHAPTER 2. IT'S A RAP

1. "Drake Gives High School Graduation Speech," Rap-Up, October 27, 2012, https://www.rap-up.com/2012/10/27/drake-gives-high-school-graduation-speech/.

CHAPTER 3. KEEP IT COMING

1. HP Cheung, "10 Things You Should Know About Drake's 'More Life,'" Hypebeast, March 20, 2017, https://hypebeast.com/2017/3/drake-more-life-album-facts-things-to-know.

2. Drake (@Drake), "Live without pretending, Love without depending, Listen without defending, Speak without offending," Twitter, February 20, 2011, 10:14 p.m., https://twitter.com/drake/status/39568541719986176.

CHAPTER 4. DOING BUSINESS AND GIVING BACK

1. "30 Drake Lyrics That Will Give You All the Feels," Capital Xtra, accessed September 24, 2018, https://www.capitalxtra.com/artists/drake/lists/emotional-lyrics/.

2. Chabeli Herrera, "Drake Had Almost $1 Million to Spend on a Music Video. He Gave It All to Miami," *Miami Herald*, February 16, 2018, https://www.miamiherald.com/entertainment/article200517604.html.

WORDS TO KNOW

album A group of songs, given as a single item.

bar mitzvah A Jewish ceremony for boys at age thirteen that celebrates their coming of age.

dancehall A type of popular music from Jamaica.

divorce The legal end of marriage.

invest To put money into something, such as a company, in hopes of earning more money.

mixtape A collection of songs recorded by rappers and DJs, usually either given away for free or sold at a low cost.

rap A kind of music with fast words said to rhythm and with instruments behind it.

rhythm A pattern of sounds, musical notes, and words.

rhythm and blues (R&B) A type of popular music invented by African Americans with blues and jazz elements.

Spotify A streaming music service.

LEARN MORE

BOOKS

Isbell, Hannah. *Drake: Actor and Rapper*. New York, NY: Enslow Publishing, 2017.

Lajiness, Katie. *Drake: Famous Music Star*. Minneapolis, MN: Big Buddy Books, 2018.

Morse, Eric. *What Is Hip-Hop?* Brooklyn, NY: Akashic Books, 2017.

WEBSITES

Drake
drakeofficial.com
Visit Drake's official website for music, videos, tour dates, merchandise, and more.

Kidzworld
www.kidzworld.com/article/5321-pioneers-of-hip-hop
Find out how hip-hop and rap got started.

INDEX